SONGS

FOR THE

WORLD

HYMNS BY CHARLES WESLEY

SINGER'S EDITION

S T KIMBROUGH, JR.
General Editor

CARLTON R. YOUNG
Music Editor

Scripture passages quoted in *Songs for the World: Singer's Edition* are from the Authorized (King James) Version of 1611, with some adjustments.

Printed in the United States of America.

Title: *Songs for the World: Singer's Edition*

ISBN 1-890569-42-9

Cover design: Trevor O'Neill, Angel Graphics

The songs in this book have been recorded by the General Board of Global Ministries, GBGMusik, under the title *Songs for the World*.

Order CD 1-015 from:

COKESBURY
201 8th Ave., South
Nashville, TN 37202
Tel. 1-800-672-1789

SERVICE CENTER
7820 Reading Road
Cincinnati, OH 45222-1800
1-800-305-9857

GBGMusik, Room 350
475 Riverside Drive
New York, NY 10115
1-212-870-3633

Acknowledgments

Deep appreciation is expressed to Dr. Carlton R. Young, music consultant for the General Board of Global Ministries, for his excellent work as the music editor and expertise in preparing the musical scores of all the hymns which appear here. In addition, sincere gratitude is expressed to the composers who willingly donated their services to contribute interesting compositions which will benefit the work of The Charles Wesley Society whose goal is the preservation, dissemination, and interpretation of the works of Charles Wesley: Ludmila Garbuzova (Russia), Per Harling (Sweden), Ivor H. Jones (United Kingdom), Mary K. Jackson, (USA), S T Kimbrough, Jr. (USA), Timothy E. Kimbrough (USA), Daud Kosasih (Indonesia), Jorge Lockward (Dominican Republic), I-to Loh (Taiwan), Jane Marshall (USA), Mark A. Miller (USA), Patrick Matsikenyiri (Zimbabwe), Simei Monteiro (Brazil), George Mulrain (Trinidad and Tobago), Joyce Sohl (USA), Pablo Sosa (Argentina). The settings of Carlton R. Young (USA) were composed for a conference on "John Wesley and the Poor" ("Happy the multitude") held at Perkins School of Theology in Dallas, Texas, and for the World Methodist Conference 2001 ("Author of our salvation, thee") in Brighton, UK. Thanks is also expressed to Mark McGurty for technical and editorial assistance.

Contributors

Ludmila Garbuzova (Russia)	I-to Loh (Taiwan)
Per Harling (Sweden)	Jane Marshall (USA)
Mary K. Jackson (USA)	Patrick Matsikenyiri (Zimbabwe)
Ivor H. Jones (United Kingdom)	Simei Monteiro (Brazil)
S T Kimbrough, Jr. (USA)	George Mulrain (Trinidad & Tobago)
Timothy E. Kimbrough (USA)	Joyce Sohl (USA)
Daud Kosasih (Indonesia)	Pablo Sosa (Argentina)
Jorge Lockward (Dominican Republic)	Carlton R. Young (USA)

Contents

Preface

This songbook grew out of discussions with leaders of The Charles Wesley Society in reference to its annual meeting for 2001 with the theme "Indigenization, Localization, and Translation of the Charles Wesley Corpus." The Wesley hymns continue to have a tremendous impact within the Christian community around the world, both individually and corporately. The powerful imagery and language of the hymns continue to be formative for the spiritual journey of individuals and the worshipping community. While their "word content" issued from the creative pen of Charles Wesley, the impact of the hymns has been greatly enhanced by the music to which they have been set across the years. Most of the music, however, has come from the United Kingdom and continental Europe. As the Christian faith has spread around the world and the Wesley hymns have enriched the lives of Christians and seekers on many continents, the message of the hymns has remained constant, but the shape of musical expression in diverse cultures has changed tremendously.

There are some instances of the joining of indigenous tunes with Wesley texts which have been most effective, such as the use of the USA folk tune LAND OF REST with the Wesley text "O thou who this mysterious bread" in *The United Methodist Hymnal* (1989), and Lim Swee Hong's musical setting for "Still for thy lovingkindness, Lord" in the songbook *Global Praise 1*. There is, however, often a posture toward the Wesley hymns, openly expressed by some and perhaps subconsciously by others, that they are most appropriately sung to tunes of the eighteenth and nineteenth centuries. The Wesleys themselves, however, reflect a very different attitude toward the hymns they were creating. John Wesley was constantly seeking appropriate musical settings for his brother's texts, as the books of hymn tunes he published reflect. He even made marginal notes in his own copies which indicate his ongoing search for appropriate musical expression of the words.

Today the Christian faith finds expression in innumerable cultures, ethnic groups, languages, diverse musical idioms, and multiple rhythms. Charles and John Wesley discovered on board a ship to America in 1735, in the midst of a storm, as they heard some German-speaking Christians calmly singing hymns in their own language, that these people, whose language they did not understand well, were expressing a deep inner peace in the face of death that they did not possess. We too today may discover new riches of inspiration and theological understanding in the Wesley hymns as they are sung to the rhythms and musical idioms of diverse cultures. Hence, here you will find music from Africa, Asia, the Caribbean region, Europe, North and South America. May you be enriched on your journey with Christ and the church as you sing.

S T Kimbrough, Jr.,
General Editor

Hymn Tunes and Texts

In addition to the musically scored versions, the hymn texts of Charles Wesley are printed on the right-hand page for study, devotion, and meditation, and the original sources are noted at the conclusion of each hymn. Many of the hymns appear here for the first time in a musical version for singing. Eight of the texts were first published in *The Unpublished Poetry of Charles Wesley: Hymns and Poems on Holy Scripture,* vol. 2 of the 3 volume series, edited by S T Kimbrough, Jr., and Oliver A. Beckerlegge (Nashville: Abingdon/Kingswood, 1990). Two of the hymns first appeared in the Wesleys' *Hymns on the Lord's Supper* (1745). Five of the hymns are well known texts which have been sung to various tunes: "And can it be that I should gain," "Gentle Jesus, meek and mild," "Love divine, all loves excelling," "With glorious clouds encompassed round," and "Where shall my wondering soul begin." These texts appeared in published collections of the Wesleys.

It was often Charles Wesley's practice to base a hymn or poem on a specific biblical passage. Where applicable, the biblical text to which he referred precedes the hymn text. The King James Version (Authorized Version) has been used, since it was the translation generally utilized by Wesley, and often the language of his verse reflects the imagery, symbolism, metaphors, and other linguistic characteristics of that translation. A few adjustments have been made in the King James Version for the sake of inclusive language, in accordance with practices in contemporary Bible translation, especially in regard to generic nouns and pronouns.

A subject index and a bibliography of the sources of the Wesley texts used in this collection are found at the conclusion of the songbook. They are followed by indexes of first lines and meters. Other appropriate tunes may be located by referring to the metrical indexes of hymnals.

And can it be that I should gain 1

Charles Wesley, 1739

Ludmila Garbuzova
arr. Carlton R. Young

1. And can it be that I should gain an in-terest in the Sav-ior's blood? Died he for me who caused his pain, for me who him to death pur-
2. 'Tis mys-tery all: th' Im-mor-tal dies! Who can ex-plore his strange de-sign? In vain the first-born ser-aph tries to sound the depths of love di-
3. Long my im-pris-oned spir-it lay, fast bound in sin and na-ture's night; thine eye dif-fused a quick-ening ray; I woke, the dun-geon flamed with
4. No con-dem-na-tion now I dread; Je-sus, and all in him, is mine; a-live in him, my liv-ing Head, and clothed in right-eous-ness di-

And can it be that I should gain

sued? A - maz - ing love, how can it
vine. 'Tis mer - cy all! Let earth a -
light; my chains fell off, my heart was
vine, bold I ap - proach th'e - ter - nal

be that thou, my God, shouldst die for me?
dore; let an - gel minds in - quire no more.
free, I rose, went forth and fol - lowed thee.
throne, and claim the crown, through Christ my own.

A - maz - ing love, how can it be
'Tis mer - cy all! let earth a - dore;
My chains fell off, my heart was free,
Bold I ap - proach th'e - ter - nal throne,

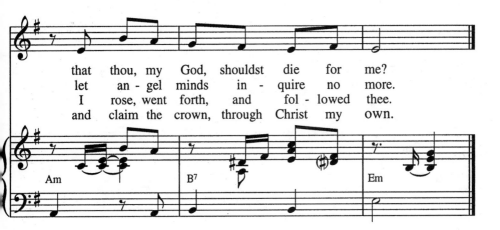

that thou, my God, shouldst die for me?
let an - gel minds in - quire no more.
I rose, went forth, and fol - lowed thee.
and claim the crown, through Christ my own.

1. And can it be that I should gain
      an interest in the Savior's blood?
   Died he for me who caused his pain,
      for me who him to death pursued?
   Amazing love, how can it be
      that thou, my God, shouldst die for me?

2. 'Tis mystery all: th'Immortal dies!
      Who can explore his strange design?
   In vain the firstborn seraph tries
      to sound the depths of love divine.
   'Tis mercy all! Let earth adore;
      let angel minds inquire no more.

3. Long my imprisoned spirit lay,
      fast bound in sin and nature's night;
   thine eye diffused a quickening ray;
      I woke, the dungeon flamed with light;
   my chains fell off, my heart was free,
      I rose, went forth, and followed thee.

4. No condemnation now I dread;
      Jesus, and all in him is mine;
   alive in him, my living Head,
      and clothed in righteousness divine,
   bold I approach th'eternal throne,
      and claim the crown, through Christ my own.

Hymns and Sacred Poems (1739): original title "Free Grace," original stanzas 1,2,4,6.

2 Author of our salvation, thee

KAREN

Charles Wesley, 1745

Carlton R. Young

1. Au - thor of our sal - va - tion, thee,
2. The sac - red, true ef - fec - tual sign
3. We see the blood that seals our peace,
4. Our spir - its drink a fresh sup - ply,

with low - ly thank - ful hearts we praise.
thy bo - dy and thy blood it shows;
thy pard' - ning mer - cy we re - ceive;
and eat the bread so free - ly given,

Au - thor of this great mys - te - ry,
the glor - ious in - stru - ment di - vine
the bread doth vis - i - bly ex - press
till borne on ea - gles wings we fly,

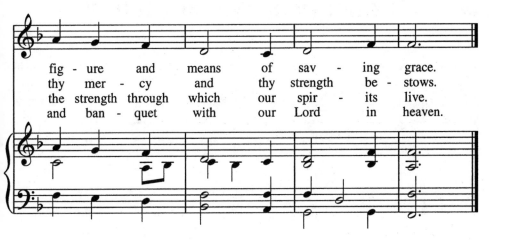

fig - ure   and   means   of   sav - ing   grace.
thy   mer - cy   and   thy   strength   be - stows.
the   strength through   which   our   spir - its   live.
and   ban - quet   with   our   Lord   in   heaven.

1. Author of our salvation, thee,
    with lowly thankful hearts we praise.
   Author of this great mystery,
    figure and means of saving grace.

2. The sacred, true effectual sign
    thy body and thy blood it shows;
   the glorious instrument divine
    thy mercy and thy strength bestows.

3. We see the blood that seals our peace,
    thy pard'ning mercy we receive;
   the bread doth visibly express
    the strength through which our spirits live.

4. Our spirits drink a fresh supply,
    and eat the bread so freely given,
   till borne on eagles wings we fly,
    and banquet with our Lord in heaven.

Hymns on the Lord's Supper (1745), No. 28, p. 22, "As it is a sign and a means of grace."

3 Father, since thou permittest

Charles Wesley

Joyce Sohl

1. Fa - ther, since thou per - mit - test a wea - ry soul's re - lease, and for thy pre - sence fit - test, I now de - part in peace. With joy - ful con - so - la - tion I out of life de -
2. Thine im - age and thy fa - vor with Je - sus is re - stored, and show - ing me my Sav - ior, thou hast per - formed thy word, hast re - com - pensed my pa - tience with Je - sus Christ, de -
3. Je - sus, thine Heir A - noint - ed, the com - mon Sav - ior is, light of the world ap - point - ed, and Is - rael's glori - ous bliss: il - lu - mined by his Spi - rit I find my way to

Music © 2001 The Charles Wesley Society, Archives and History Center, Drew University, Madison, NJ 07940; administered by General Board of Global Ministries, GBGMusik, 475 Riverside Drive, New York, NY 10115. Used by permission. All rights reserved.

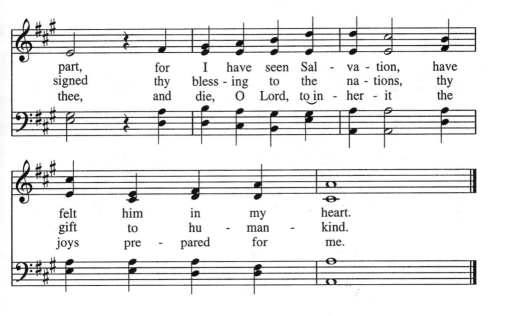

part,   for I have seen Sal - va - tion,   have
signed   thy bless - ing to the na - tions,   thy
thee,   and die, O Lord, to in - her - it   the

felt   him   in   my   heart.
gift   to   hu - man - kind.
joys   pre - pared   for   me.

Luke 2:29-32: Lord, now lettest thou thy servant depart in peace, according to thy word: for mine eyes have seen thy salvation, which thou has prepared before the face of all people; a light to lighten the Gentiles, and the glory of thy people Israel.

1. Father, since thou permittest
    a weary soul's release,
and for thy presence fittest,
    I now depart in peace.
With joyful consolation
    I out of life depart,
for I have seen Salvation,
    have felt him in my heart.

2. Thine image and thy favor
    with Jesus is restored,
and showing me my Savior,
    thou hast performed thy word,
hast recompensed my patience
    with Jesus Christ, designed
thy blessing to the nations,
    thy gift to humankind.

3. Jesus, thine Heir Anointed,
    the common Savior is,
light of the world appointed,
    and Israel's glorious bliss:
illumined by his Spirit
    I find my way to thee,
and die, O Lord, to inherit
    the joys prepared for me.

The Unpublished Poetry of Charles Wesley (1990), 2:82-83.

4 Gentle Jesus, meek and mild

Charles Wesley, 1742

I-to Loh

1. Gentle Jesus, meek and mild,
   look upon a little child,
   pity my simplicity
   suffer me to come to thee.

2. Fain I would be as thou art;
   give me thine obedient heart;
   thou art pitiful and kind;
   let me have thy loving mind.

pit - y my sim - plic - i - ty
thou art pit - i - ful and kind;
nev - er God's good Spir - it grieve,
make me, Sav - ior, what thou art;
then the world shall al - ways see

suf - fer me to come to thee.
let me have thy lov - ing mind.
on - ly to God's glo - ry live.
live thy - self with - in my heart.
Christ, the Ho - ly Child, in me.

3. Let me above all fulfill
God my heavenly Father's will;
never God's good Spirit grieve,
only to God's glory live.

4. Loving Jesus, gentle Lamb,
in thy gracious hands I am;
make me, Savior, what thou art;
live thyself within my heart.

5. I shall then show forth thy praise,
serve thee all my happy days;
then the world shall always see
Christ, the Holy Child, in me.

Hymns and Sacred Poems (1742), p. 191-192, original stanzas 1,2,11,13,14.

5 Grace our every thought controls

Charles Wesley, 1745

Simei Monteiro

1. Grace our every thought controls, heaven is opened in our souls, everlasting life is won, glory is our earth begun.
3. Him by faith we taste below, mightier joys ordained to know, when his utmost grace we prove, rise to heaven by perfect love.

2. Christ in us; in him we see fullness
4. Love's mysterious work is done; greet we

1. Grace our every thought controls,
   heaven is opened in our souls,
   everlasting life is won,
   glory is on earth begun.

2. Christ in us; in him we see
   fullness of the Deity,
   beam of the Eternal Beam;
   life divine we taste in him.

3. Him by faith we taste below,
   mightier joys ordained to know,
   when his utmost grace we prove,
   rise to heaven by perfect love.

4. Love's mysterious work is done;
   greet we now th'atoning Son,
   healed and quickened by his blood,
   joined to Christ, and one with God.

Hymns on the Lord's Supper (1745), from the section "After the Sacrament," No. 164, pp. 137-138, stanzas 6,7,8,3.

6

Hallelujah, Christ is risen

Charles Wesley
refrain, S T Kimbrough, Jr.

BAKER
S T Kimbrough, Jr.
arr. Mary K. Jackson

All voices

1. More cou - ra - geous than the men, when
2. Wo - men first the news pro - claim, know
3. Joy - ful tid - ings of their Lord these
4. O might I like them now hear, these

C   Am   F   C   F   C   Em

Christ his breath re - signed,   wo - men first the
re - sur - rec - tion's power,   teach the A - pos - tles
mes - sen - gers pro - claim   Je - sus Christ to
wit - ness - es re - ceive;   emp - ty find the

Am   G   Fm⁷   G   C   Dm

D.S. al Fine
Alto

grace ob - tain their liv - ing Lord to find. Hal - le -
of the Lamb, who lives to die no more.
life re - stored, and par - don through his name!
se - pul - chre, and won - der and be - lieve!

Dm   E   Am   C   F   G⁹   G⁷   C

Luke 24:10: It was Mary Magdalene, and Joanna, and Mary the mother of James, and other women that were with them which told these things unto the Apostles.

Refrain:
Hallelujah! Christ is risen!
Now the stone's rolled away.
Hallelujah! Christ is risen!
Proclaim the news today!

1. More courageous than the men,
when Christ his breath resigned,
women first the grace obtain
their living Lord to find.
Refrain:

2. Women first the news proclaim,
know resurrection's power,
teach th'Apostles of the Lamb,
who lives to die no more.
Refrain:

3. Joyful tidings of their Lord
these messengers proclaim
Jesus Christ to life restored,
and pardon through his name!
Refrain:

4. O might I like them now hear,
these witnesses receive;
empty find the sepulchre,
and wonder and believe!
Refrain:

Happy the multitude

Charles Wesley

Carlton R. Young

Happy the multitude

heart and mind.
ny and love.
ty Di - vine.

all pos - sessed.

Acts 4:32: The multitude of them that believed, were of one heart, and one soul; neither said any of them, that aught of the things which he possessed, was his own, but they had all things common. Neither was there any among them that had lacked.

1. Happy the multitude
    (but far above our sphere)
   redeemed by Jesus' blood
       from all we covet here!
   To him, and to each other joined,
   they all were of one heart and mind.

2. His blood the cement was
       who died on Calvary,
   and fastened to his cross
       they could not disagree:
   one soul did all the members move,
   the soul of harmony and love.

3. Their goods were free for all,
       appropriated to none,
   while none presumed to call
       what he possessed his own;
   the difference-base of *thine* and *mine*
   was lost with charity divine.

4. No overplus, or need,
       no rich or poor were there,
   content with daily bread
       where all enjoyed their share;
   with every common blessing blessed
   they nothing had, yet all possessed.

The Unpublished Poetry of Charles Wesley (1990), 2:295-296.

8   He did not proclaim

Charles Wesley

Per Harling

♩ = 96

1. He did not pro - claim to all that passed by, "How
2. The gift who re - ceives, and has - tens to tell he
3. The grace I have found, O Je - sus, with thee, I
4. Of par - don pos - sessed, my God I a - dore; yet
5. The grace to in - sure, the trea - sure con - cealed, a

hap - py I am, how sanc - ti - fied I!" But
calls on the thieves his trea - sure to steal: Who
hide in the ground for no man to see: The
can I not rest, im - pa - tient for more; a
men - di - cant poor I pur - chase the field, sell

find - ing a mea - sure of heav - en - ly power, con -
vain - ly re - fus - es, or lin - gers to hide, his
grace I con - fide in, the trea - sure thou art, who
great - er sal - va - tion I lan - guish to prove, a
all to ob - tain it, and seek till I find, and

cealed the rich trea-sure, and la-bored for more.
rich-es he los-es through fol-ly and pride.
lov'st to re-side in a pen-i-tent heart.
deep-er foun-da-tion, a sol-id-er love.
ask, till I gain it in Je-sus his mind.

Matthew 13:44: The kingdom of heaven is like unto treasure hid in a field, which when a man hath found, he hideth, and for joy thereof goeth and selleth all that he hath, and buyeth that field.

1. He did not proclaim to all that passed by,
   "How happy I am, how sanctified I!"
   But finding a measure of heavenly power,
   concealed the rich treasure, and labored for more.

2. The gift who receives, and hastens to tell
   he calls on the thieves his treasure to steal:
   Who vainly refuses, or lingers to hide,
   his riches he loses through folly and pride.

3. The grace I have found, O Jesus, with thee,
   I hide in the ground for no one to see:
   The grace I confide in, the treasure thou art,
   who lov'st to reside in a penitent heart.

4. Of pardon possessed, my God I adore;
   yet can I not rest, impatient for more;
   a greater salvation I languish to prove,
   a deeper foundation, a solider love.

5. The grace to insure, the treasure concealed,
   a mendicant poor I purchase the field,
   sell all to obtain it, and seek till I find,
   and ask, till I gain it in Jesus his mind.

The Unpublished Poetry of Charles Wesley (1990), 2:29.

9   In my last distress

OUTLER
Jane Marshall

Charles Wesley

1. In my last dis-tress re-lieve me: God un-known, thou a-lone
2. Pros-trate in the dust, and cry-ing af-ter thee, Mer-cy, see,

canst, and wilt for-give me; by thy Spir-it's in-spir-a-tion
see my soul a-dy-ing. Save the con-scious un-be-liev-er,

faith im-part, tell my heart, "I am thy sal-va-tion."
save, or I faint and die, die, un-done for-ev-er.

Performance note: It is recommended that stanza 1 be repeated after stanza 2.

Acts 26:15: "Who art thou, Lord?"

1. In my last distress relieve me:
        God unknown,
        thou alone
    canst, and wilt forgive me;
   by thy Spirit's inspiration
        faith impart,
        tell my heart,
    "I am thy salvation."

2. Prostrate in the dust and crying
        after thee,
        Mercy, see,
    see my soul a-dying.
   Save the conscious unbeliever,
        save, or I
        faint and die,
    die, undone for ever.

The Unpublished Poetry of Charles Wesley (1990), 2:428.

10 Now, ev'n now, the kingdom's near

Charles Wesley

George Mulrain
arr. Jorge Lockward

* Performance notes: "Even now" is suggested as an alternative to "Now e'ven now." It is recommen
that stanza 1 be repeated after stanza 2.

Luke 19:11: They thought that the kingdom of God should immediately appear.

1. Now, ev'n now, the kingdom's near,
   peace and joy, and righteousness,
soon it shall in us appear;
   reverent joy, victorious peace.
Real righteousness brought in
   roots out selfishness and pride,
finishes the inbred sin,
   makes us like the Crucified.

2. Nature cannot comprehend
   Jesus reigning on the cross,
that he may on him depend,
   suffering, dying in his cause;
nature would in pomp and state
   high at his right-hand sit down,
suddenly be rich and great,
   shun the cross, but snatch the crown.

The Unpublished Poetry of Charles Wesley (1990), 2:174.

11   O Jesus, in thee my salvation I see

Charles Wesley

Mary K. Jackson

♩. = 44-48

1. O Jesus, in thee my salvation I see,
thy presence confess most near to assist in my greatest distress. In the gloom-i-est hour sus-tained by thy power, and re-vived by thy

2. I both see thee and hear in-ex-pres-sib-ly near to de-liv-er thine own, and to com-fort my heart in a man-ner un-known. But be-liev-ers can tell what an heav-en I feel, when thou bidst me pur-

3. Thy mes-sen-ger, I, on the prom-ise re-ly of thy pres-ence be-low, to up-hold me and guide where-so-ev-er I go: and I on-ly would live my whole wit-ness to give, and in ev-e-ry

Music © 2001 The Charles Wesley Society, Archives and History Center, Drew University, Madison, NJ 07940; administered by General Board of Global Ministries, GBGMusik, 475 Riverside Drive, New York, NY 10115. Used by permission. All rights reserved.

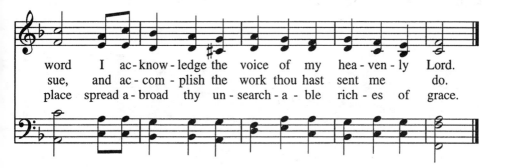

word   I ac-know-ledge the voice of my hea-ven-ly Lord.
sue,   and ac-com-plish the work thou hast sent me   do.
place spread a-broad thy un-search-a-ble rich-es of grace.

Acts 23:11: And the night following, the Lord stood by him, and said, Be of good cheer, Paul: for as thou hast testified of me in Jerusalem, so must thou bear witness also at Rome.

1.   O Jesus, in thee
      my salvation I see,
      thy presence confess
  most near to assist in my greatest distress.
      In the gloomiest hour
      sustained by thy power,
      and revived by thy word
  I acknowledge the voice of my heavenly Lord.

2.   I both see thee and hear
      inexpressibly near
      to deliver thine own,
  and to comfort my heart in a manner unknown.
      But believers can tell
      what an heaven I feel,
      when thou bidst me pursue,
  and accomplish the work thou hast sent me to do.

3.   Thy messenger, I,
      on the promise rely
      of thy presence below,
  to uphold me and guide wheresoever I go:
      and I only would live
      my whole witness to give,
      and in every place
  spread abroad thy unsearchable riches of grace.

The Unpublished Poetry of Charles Wesley (1990), 2:414.

12 With glorious clouds encompassed round

WESLEY HOUSE
Ivor H. Jones

Charles Wesley, 1767

1. With glor - ious clouds en - com - pass'd round, whom an - gels dim - ly see,
2. In man - i - fest - ed love ex - plain the won - der - ful de - sign:
3. Come then, and to my soul re - veal the heights and depths of grace,

will the Un - search - a - ble be found, or
What meant the suf - fering Son of Man, the
the wounds which all my sor - rows heal, that

God ap - pear to me? Will he for - sake his
stream - ing love di - vine? Didst thou not in our
dear dis - fig - ured face, I view the Lamb in

throne a-bove, him-self to me im-part?
flesh ap-pear, and live and die be-low,
his own light, whom an-gels dim-ly see,

An-swer, thou Man of grief and love, and speak it to my heart!
that I may now per-ceive thee near, and my Re-deem-er know?
and gaze, trans-port-ed at the sight, through all e-ter-ni-ty.

1. With glorious clouds encompassed round,
    whom angels dimly see,
will the Unsearchable be found,
    or God appear to me?
Will he forsake his throne above,
    himself to me impart?
Answer, thou Man of grief and love,
    and speak it to my heart!

2. In manifested love explain
    thy wonderful design:
What meant the suffering Son of Man,
    the streaming blood divine?
Didst thou not in our flesh appear,
    and live and die below,
that I may now perceive thee near,
    and my Redeemer know?

3. Come then, and to my soul reveal
    the heights and depths of grace,
the wounds which all my sorrows heal,
    that dear disfigured face.
I view the Lamb in his own light,
    whom angels dimly see,
and gaze, transported at the sight,
    through all eternity.

Hymns for Use of Families, and on Various Occasions (1767), stanzas 1-5, 8.

13 Come to the Supper

For SATB voices

Charles Wesley, 1745

Patrick Matsikenyiri
transc. Mark McGurty

♩ = 132

T. Come to the ta-ble, come to the ta-ble, come to the ta-ble,

B. Come to the ta-ble, come to the ta-ble, come to the ta-ble, come to the ta-ble.

S. 1. Come to the Sup-per, (the Sup-per), come, sin - ners there still is

A. 1. Come to the Sup-per, (the Sup-per), come, sin - ners there still is

T. Come to the ta - ble, come to the ta-ble, come to the ta-ble.

B. Come to the ta - ble, come to the ta-ble, come to the ta-ble,

room, there's room; ev - ery soul may be his guest,

room, there's room; ev - ery soul may be his guest,

Come to the ta - ble, come to the ta-ble,

come to the ta - ble. Come to the ta - ble, come to the ta-ble,

Come to the Supper

Performance note: The soprano and alto parts may be sung without the tenor and bass parts, beginning at line 2 on the first page and concluding at the last measure of the third page. Shakers and drums may also be added as rhythm instruments.

1. Come to the Supper, come,
     sinners there still is room;
   every soul may be his guest,
     Jesus gives the gen'ral word.
   Share the monumental feast,
     eat the Supper of your Lord.

2. In this authentic sign
     behold the stamp divine.
   Christ revives his sufferings here,
     still exposes them to view;
   see the Crucified appear,
     now believe he died for you!

Hymns on the Lord's Supper (1745), No. 8, p. 7.

14   O gentle Shepherd, hear my cry

Charles Wesley

Jorge A. Lockward

1. O gentle Shepherd, hear my cry, and hark-en as thou pas-sest by
2. Come, lead me forth to pas-tures green, to fer-tile meads, where all se-rene
3. O God, thy prom-ised aid im-part, con-vert my soul and change my heart,
4. When through the gloom-y shade I roam, pale death's dark vail, to end-less home,
5. Though foes sur-round, be-fore their face pre-pare a ta-ble decked with grace,
6. A pil-grim whilst on earth I rove, O let me all thy good-ness prove;

O gentle Shepherd, hear my cry

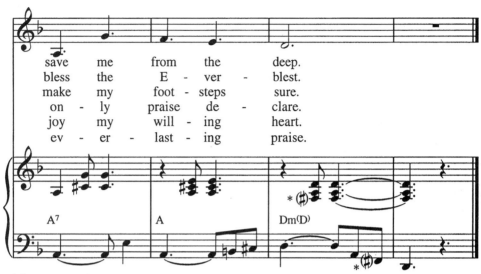

* Last stanza only.

1. O gentle Shepherd, hear my cry,
   and harken as thou passest by
      to a poor wand'ring sheep;
   relieve me with thy tender care,
   behold my want of help; draw near
      and save me from the deep.

2. Come, lead me forth to pastures green,
   to fertile meads, where all serene
      invites to peace and rest;
   near the still waters let me lie,
   to view them gently murmur by,
      then bless the Ever-blest.

3. O God, thy promised aid impart,
   convert my soul and change my heart,
      and make my nature pure;
   come, change my nature into thine;
   still lead me in the path divine,
      and make my footsteps sure.

4. When through the gloomy shade I roam,
   pale death's dark vale, to endless home,
      O save me then from fear;
   vouchsafe with love my soul to fill,
   that I in death may fear no ill,
      and only praise declare.

5. Though foes surround, before their face
   prepare a table decked with grace,
      thy food, O Lord, impart;
   with sacred oil anoint my head,
   and let thy mighty love o'erspread
      with joy my willing heart.

6. A pilgrim whilst on earth I rove,
   O let me all thy goodness prove;
      let mercy end my days;
   admit, at last, my wandering feet
   thy courts to enter, thee to greet
      with everlasting praise.

The Unpublished Poetry of Charles Wesley (1990), 2:441-442.

Whither should our full souls aspire 15

Unison anthem or solo with keyboard accompaniment

Charles Wesley, 1745

HILLSBOROUGH
Timothy E. Kimbrough

Performance note: Stanza 4 is sung twice in this setting: once after stanza 2, and again after stanza 3.

Whither should our full souls aspire

Whither should our full souls aspire

Dal segno al Coda ⊕ Coda

en – ter   in - to   their   Mas – ter's

B♭   B♭7(♭9)   Adim   *cresc.*   D   Gm⁹

rubato

bliss   and   feast   for – ev – er   there._____

Gm⁷/F   E♭   Cm   Cm⁷/F

a tempo

4. To heaven   the   mys – tic   ban – quet

f   B♭Maj⁷   Fm/A♭   B♭/G

1. Whither should our full souls aspire
   at this transporting feast?
   They never can on earth be higher,
   or more completely blest.

2. Our cup of blessing from above
   delightfully runs o'er,
   till from our bodies they remove
   our souls can hold no more.

3. Till all who truly join in this,
   the Marriage-Supper share,
   enter into their Master's bliss
   and feast for ever there.

4. To heaven the mystic banquet lead
   let us to heaven ascend
   and bear this joy upon our heads
   till in glory end.

Hymns on the Lord's Supper (1745), No. 99 in the section 3, "The Sacrament a Pledge of Heaven."

Stranger unknown, thou art my God

Luke 10:34-35: He went to him, and bound up his wounds, pouring in oil and wine, and set him on his own beast, and brought him to an inn, and took care of him. And on the morrow when he departed, he took out two pence, and gave them to the host, and said unto him, Take care of him; and whatsoever thou spendest more, when I come again, I will repay thee.

1. Stranger unknown, thou art my God!
   From me, while weltring in my blood,
   thou canst not farther go.
   Pour in thy Spirit's wine and oil,
   revive me by a gracious smile,
   thy pard'ning mercy show.

2. Bind up my wounds by opening thin
   apply the balm of blood divine
   to save a sinner poor;
   to life, and joy, and gospel-peace
   (sure pledge of perfect holiness)
   my gasping soul restore.

3. Thy patient in thy hands I lie,
   all helplessness, all weakness I,
   but thy almighty skill
   on sinners to the utmost showed,
   shall through the virtue of the blood
   my soul completely heal.

The Unpublished Poetry of Charles Wesley (1990), 2:122-123.

Stranger unknown

Charles Wesley

Pablo Sosa

1. Strang er un - known, thou art my God!
3. Thy pa - tient in thy hands I lie,

From me, while wel - - tring
all help - less - ness, all

Stranger unknown

Where shall my wondering soul begin? 17

Charles Wesley, 1739

Daud Kosasih

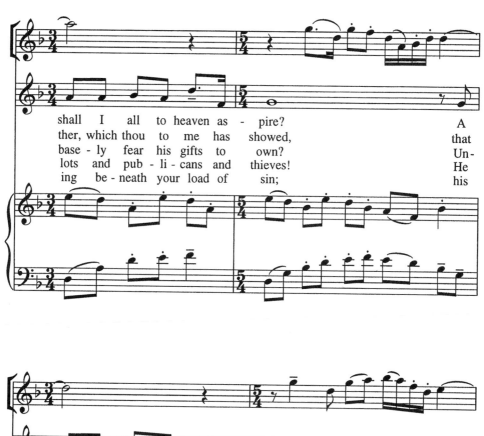

shall   I   all   to heaven as - pire?
ther, which thou   to   me has   showed,
base - ly   fear   his gifts   to   own?
lots   and   pub - li - cans and   thieves!
ing   be - neath   your load of   sin;

A
that
Un -
He
his

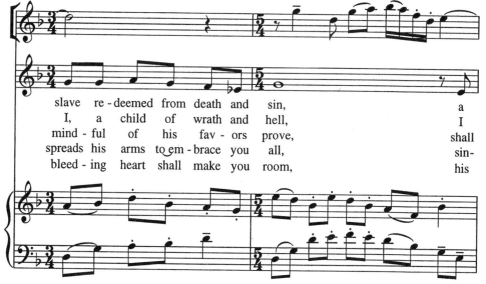

slave   re - deemed   from death and   sin,
I,   a   child   of   wrath and   hell,
mind - ful   of   his   fav - ors   prove,
spreads his   arms to em - brace you   all,
bleed - ing   heart shall   make you   room,

a
I
shall
sin-
his

brand plucked from e - ter - nal fire,   how
should   be   called   a   child   of   God!   Should
I,   the   hallow - ed   cross   to   shun,   re -
ners   a - lone   his   grace   re - ceives.   No
o - pen   side   shall   take   you   in.   He

shall   I   e - qual   tri - umphs   raise,   or
know, should   feel   my   sins   for - given,   blest
fuse   his   righ - teous - ness   to im - part,   by
need   of   him   the   righ - teous   have;   he
calls   you   now,   in - vites   you   home: Come,

Where shall my wondering soul begin?

1. Where shall my wondering soul begin?
    How shall I all to heaven aspire?
A slave redeemed from death and sin,
    a brand plucked from eternal fire,
how shall I equal triumphs raise,
or sing my great deliverer's praise?

2. O how shall I the goodness tell,
    Father, which thou to me hast showed,
that I, a child of wrath and hell,
    I should be called a child of God!
Should know, should feel my sins forgiven,
blest with this antepast of heaven!

Where shall my wondering soul begin?

sing my great de-li-ver's praise?
with this ant-e-past of heaven!
hid-ing it with-in my heart?
came the lost to seek and save.
O my guilt-y sin-ners, come.

3. And shall I slight my Father's love,
   or basely fear his gifts to own?
   Unmindful of his favors prove,
   shall I, the hallowed cross to shun,
   refuse his righteousness to impart,
   by hiding it within my heart?

4. Outcasts of earth, to you I call,
   harlots and publicans and thieves!
   He spreads his arms to embrace you all,
   sinners alone his grace receives.
   No need of him the righteous have;
   he came the lost to seek and save.

5. Come, O my guilty sinners, come,
   groaning beneath your load of sin;
   his bleeding heart shall make you room,
   his open side shall take you in.
   He calls you now, invites you home:
   Come, O my guilty sinners, come.

Hymns and Sacred Poems (1739), original title:"Christ the Friend of Sinners," original stanzas 1,2,3,5,7.

Love divine, all loves excelling 18

Unison anthem or solo with keyboard accompaniment

Charles Wesley, 1747

Mark A. Miller

1. Love di - vine, all loves ex - cell - ing, joy of heaven to earth come down;
2. Breathe, O breathe thy lov - ing Spir - it in - to ev - ery trou - bled breast!
3. Fin - ish, then, thy new cre - a - tion; pure and spot - less let us be.

fix in us__ Let us all__ Let us see__

Love divine, all loves excelling

Love divine, all loves excelling

1. Love divine, all loves excelling,
     joy of heaven to earth come down;
fix in us thy humble dwelling;
     all thy faithful mercies crown!
Jesus, thou art all compassion,
     pure, unbounded love thou art;
visit us with thy salvation;
     enter every trembling heart.

2. Breathe, O breathe thy loving Spirit
     into every troubled breast!
Let us all in thee inherit;
     let us find that second rest.
Thee we would be always blessing,
     serve thee as thy host above,
pray and praise thee without ceasing,
     glory in thy perfect love.

3. Finish, then, thy new creation;
     pure and spotless let us be.
Let us see thy great salvation
     perfectly restored in thee;
changed from glory into glory,
     till in heaven we take our place,
till we cast our crowns before thee,
     lost in wonder, love, and praise.

Hymns for those that seek and those that have Redemption in the Blood of Jesus Christ (1747), No. 9, pp. 11-12.

Subject Index

Index of First Lines and Meters

Bibliography of Sources of Wesley Hymn Texts

John and Charles Wesley, *Hymns on the Lord's Supper*, Bristol: Farley, 1745.

John and Charles Wesley, *Hymns and Sacred Poems,* London: Strahan, 1739.

John and Charles Wesley, *Hymns and Sacred Poems,* Bristol: Farley, 1742.

Charles Wesley, *Hymns for the Use of Families and on Various Occasions,* Bristol: Pine, 1767.

Charles Wesley, *Hymns for those that seek and those that have Redemption in the Blood of Jesus Christ*, London: Strahan, 1747.

S T Kimbrough, Jr. and Oliver A. Beckerlegge, *The Unpublished Poetry of Charles Wesley: Hymns and Poems on Holy Scripture,* vol. 2, Nashville: Abingdon Press, 1990.